Tai Ji Dancing for Kids

by the same author

The Chinese Book of Animal Powers
ISBN 978 1 84819 066 5
eISBN 978 0 85701 037 7

Embrace Tiger, Return to Mountain
The Essence of Tai Ji
Photographs by Si Chi Ko
ISBN 978 1 84819 052 8
eISBN 978 0 85701 038 4

Essential Tai Ji
Photographs by Si Chi Ko
ISBN 978 1 84819 053 5
eISBN 978 0 85701 035 3

Quantum Soup
Fortune Cookies in Crisis
ISBN 978 1 84819 054 2
eISBN 978 0 85701 036 0

Tai Ji Dancing for Kids

Chungliang Al Huang

with
Lark Huang-Storms
& Sylvia Yulan Storms

SINGING
DRAGON

LONDON AND PHILADELPHIA

When children move, they are naturally full of energetic life force. In Chinese, we call this Qi (Chi), which is everywhere, vibrantly alive and moving through us. When we do Tai Ji, our Qi connects us to each other and nature's energy all around us.

These movements usually flow from one to the next while you enjoy deep breathing and a calm bright mind. Some people repeat the sequence a few times at a slower rhythm, and others like to improvise and wiggle. The Qi flows however you move, and it's all the better if you are laughing! Try adding music!

For a video link to see more Tai Ji dancing, go to
www.jkp.com/catalogue/book/9781848193727
and livingtao.org/videos/five-moving-forces

Breathe into your Belly...
Feel the EARTH under
your feet

3

Open your arms
Open your eyes
Open your flowering Heart

Open your arms to the Sky
Let the sun shine in!

Pump up the EARTH energy

9

Push the FIRE out and UP!

Let the **WATER** flow down...
...AHHHHHHHHH!

Be a **TREE** branching out
looking all around you

Scoop in the GOLD
Scoop in the Jewels

Collect them into your Heart

Feel the power in your Belly

Drop it down and let it all go
Feel light and free

Jump up and take Flight!

Hug your Tiger!
Look into its eyes and
growwwl!

Settle back down
Feet on the ground
Happy Landing

Let's do it again!

A grandpa and granddaughter
collaboration

Five Moving Forces

EARTH   

FIRE

WATER

WOOD

GOLD

I grew up experiencing this magical energy as a child in rural China. I danced with nature and followed its movements. Only later, in cities with grown-ups, I realized it was called Tai Ji.

After I came to America to study and decided to live in the West, I was fortunate enough to become a Tai Ji master, and now teach people all over the world, writing books and creating videos for people of all ages.

I have found in my granddaughter Sylvie the same joy and spontaneity I experienced as a child. I shared with her the basic understandings and invited her to dance Tai Ji with me. Her mom, Lark, took some photos and I painted some Chinese calligraphy to make this book. We wish to share this connection with other children and their loved grown-ups, to have the same joyful fun experience together.

— Chungliang

*I hope you enjoy Tai Ji
dancing together!*

—Sylvie

First published in 2018
by Singing Dragon
an imprint of Jessica Kingsley Publishers
73 Collier Street
London N1 9BE, UK
and
400 Market Street, Suite 400
Philadelphia, PA 19106, USA

www.singingdragon.com

Library of Congress Cataloging in Publication Data
A CIP catalog record for this book is available from the Library of Congress

British Library Cataloguing in Publication Data
A CIP catalogue record for this book is available from the British Library

ISBN 978 1 84819 372 7
eISBN 978 0 85701 329 3

Printed and bound in China